may you find many moments of joy and pleasure reading this book. Merry Christmas Arlene. Love, Louise 1980

PROMISES
OF
JESUS

Christian Herald Books
40 Overlook Drive, Chappaqua, New York 10514

Kept by God

All that the Father gives me will come to me, and whoever comes to me I will never drive away. For I have come down from heaven not to do my will but to do the will of him who sent me. And this is the will of him who

sent me, that I shall lose none of all that he has given me, but raise them up at the last day. For my Father's will is that everyone who looks to the Son and believes in him shall have eternal life, and I will raise him up at the last day.

John 6:37–40

A child, held safe in a pannier, returns from the fields with her father.

Real happiness

Looking at his disciples, Jesus said:

'Blessed are you who are poor,
for yours is the kingdom of God.
Blessed are you who hunger now,
for you will be satisfied.

Blessed are you who weep now,
for you will laugh.
Blessed are you when men hate you,
when they exclude you and insult you
and reject your name as evil,
because of the Son of Man.
Rejoice in that day and leap for joy,
because great is your reward in heaven.'

Luke 6:20–23

A group of happy children in Jerusalem.

God
will provide

Do not set your heart on what you will eat or drink; do not worry about it. For the pagan world runs after all such things, and your Father knows that you need them. But seek his kingdom, and these things will be given to you as well.

Luke 12:29–31

Food on display in a market at Bergama (ancient Pergamum) in Turkey.

Living bread

I tell you the truth, he who believes
has everlasting life. I am the bread of
life. Your forefathers ate the manna in
the desert, yet they died. But there is
the bread that comes down from

heaven, which a man may eat and not die. I am the living bread that came down from heaven. If a man eats of this bread, he will live for ever. This bread is my flesh, which I will give for the life of the world.

John 6:47–51

A Bedouin woman in Jordan bakes unleavened bread.

God's infinite care

Are not two sparrows sold for a penny? Yet not one of them will fall to the ground apart from the will of your Father. And even the very hairs of your head are all numbered.

Matthew 10:29–30

A place prepared

Do not let your hearts be troubled. Trust in God; trust also in me. In my Father's house are many rooms; if it were not so, I would have told you. I am going there to prepare a place for you. And if I go and prepare a place for you, I will come back and take you to be with me that you also may be where I am.

John 14:1–3

A scene of tropical beauty, beside Lake Galilee.

17

Rest

Come to me, all you who are weary
and burdened, and I will give you
rest. Take my yoke upon you and
learn from me, for I am gentle and
humble in heart, and you will find
rest for your souls. For my yoke is
easy and my burden is light.

Matthew 11:28–30

A Turkish farmer rests from his work.

'A hundred times as much'

I tell you the truth . . . no-one who has left home or brothers or sisters or mother or father or children or fields for me and the gospel will fail to receive a hundred times as much in this present age (homes, brothers, sisters, mothers, children and fields – and with them, persecutions) and in the age to come, eternal life.

Mark 10:29–30

Gathering in a rich harvest.

Faith

When they came to the crowd, a man approached Jesus and knelt before him. 'Lord, have mercy on my son,' he said. 'He is an epileptic and is suffering greatly. He often falls into the fire or into the water. I brought him to your disciples, but they could not heal him.'

'O unbelieving and perverse generation,' Jesus replied, 'how long shall I stay with you? How long shall I put up with you? Bring the boy here to me.' Jesus rebuked the demon, and

it came out of the boy, and he was
healed from that moment.

Then the disciples came to Jesus in
private and asked, 'Why couldn't we
drive it out?'

He replied, 'Because you have so little
faith. I tell you the truth, if you have
faith as small as a mustard seed, you
can say to this mountain, "Move from
here to there" and it will move.
Nothing will be impossible for you.'

Matthew 17:14–20

The distant mountains are Mt Gerizim and Mt Ebal
in 'Samaria'.

Whatever you ask for

Whatever you ask for in prayer,
believe that you have received it, and
it will be yours.

Mark 11:24

Safe
in God's care

My sheep listen to my voice; I know them, and they follow me. I give them eternal life, and they shall never perish; no-one can snatch them out of my hand. My Father, who has given them to me, is greater than all; no-one can snatch them out of my Father's hand. I and the Father are one.

John 10:27–30

A shepherd watches over his flock of sheep.

God's measure

Do not judge, and you will not be judged. Do not condemn, and you will not be condemned. Forgive, and you will be forgiven. Give, and it will be given to you. A good measure, pressed down, shaken together and running over, will be poured into your lap. For with the measure you use, it will be measured to you.

Luke 6:37–38

Beans and nuts sold by measure in the market at Nazareth.

Life-giving water

Everyone who drinks this water will be thirsty again, but whoever drinks the water I give him will never thirst. Indeed, the water I give him will become in him a spring of water welling up to eternal life.

John 4:13–14

A pool of water from the spring at Engedi, Israel.

The food that lasts

Do not work for food that spoils, but for food that endures to eternal life, which the Son of Man will give you. On him God the Father has placed his seal of approval.

John 6:27

A Jewish meal being enjoyed out of doors.

'My servant'

I tell you the truth, unless an ear of
wheat falls to the ground and dies, it
remains only a single seed. But if it
dies, it produces many seeds. The
man who loves his life will lose it,
while the man who hates his life in
this world will keep it for eternal life.
Whoever serves me must follow me;
and where I am, my servant also will
be. My Father will honour the one
who serves me.

John 12:24–26

God's
promised power

This is what is written: The Christ will suffer and rise from the dead on the third day, and repentance and forgiveness of sins will be preached in his name to all nations, beginning at Jerusalem. You are witnesses of these things. I am going to send you what my Father has promised; but stay in the city until you have been clothed with power from on high.

Luke 24:46–49

Looking towards the city of Jerusalem.

All truth

When he, the Spirit of truth, comes,
he will guide you into all truth. He
will not speak on his own; he will
speak only what he hears, and he will
tell you what is yet to come.

John 16:13

A candle illuminates the Scriptures.

'I will
come to you'

I will not leave you as orphans; I will
come to you. Before long, the world
will not see me any more, but you will
see me. Because I live, you also will
live. On that day you will realise that I
am in my Father, and you are in me,
and I am in you.

John 14:18–20

Sunrise on Lake Galilee.

Jesus' promise from the cross

One of the criminals who hung there hurled insults at him: 'Aren't you the Christ? Save yourself and us!'

But the other criminal rebuked him. 'Don't you fear God,' he said, 'since you are under the same sentence? We are punished justly, for we are getting what our deeds deserve. But this man has done nothing wrong.' Then he said, 'Jesus, remember me when you come into your kingdom.'

Jesus answered him, 'I tell you the truth, today you will be with me in paradise.'

Luke 23:39–43

The words of Jesus

Heaven and earth will pass away, but my words will never pass away.

Luke 21:33